USBORNE
24 Hours in the Jungle

Lan Cook

Illustrated by Stacey Thomas

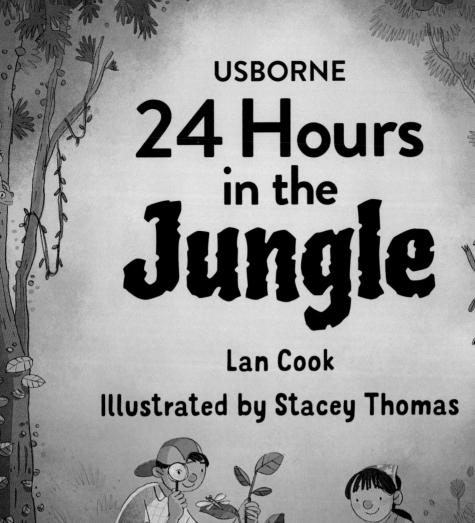

Designed by Tom Ashton-Booth
Consultant: Professor Owen Lewis

Owen Lewis is Professor of Ecology at the University of Oxford and a
Fellow of Brasenose College. With his research group and many international
collaborators, he studies the extraordinary plant and animal diversity of
tropical rainforests and how they are impacted by humans.

Usborne Quicklinks

For links to websites and videos where you can find out
more about life in the Jungle, go to usborne.com/Quicklinks
and type in the title of this book.

Here are some of the things you can do at
the websites we recommend:

- Discover amazing facts about orangutans
- Cruise along a river in Borneo
- Watch a stinking corpse lily bloom
- Find out how to make a moth trap
- See wild animals filmed at camera traps in Borneo
- Make a field journal and record wildlife where you live

Please follow the online safety guidelines at Usborne Quicklinks.
Children should be supervised online. Usborne Publishing is not
responsible for the content of external websites.

CONTENTS

Southeast Asia,
the island of Borneo...

...a new day breaks and the
jungle begins to come alive.

Insects chirp and buzz, birds
sing and gibbons begin their
morning call.

Sound fills the jungle.

HOH HOH HOH HOH...

Red-naped
trogon

KRA! KRA!

Rhinoceros
hornbill

HOOOO WOOP...

SKREEE

WA WUH WAWAWAWA...

SKREEE

Green
broadbill

...WOOP WOOP
WOOOOOP!

HOOOO WOO...

WOO OOO WOO OOO

WOOOOP WOO WOO

Müller's
gibbon

HOO HOOO!

SKREEE

Kinabatangan
River

Brown pansy
butterfly

SKREEE

SKREE

Cicada
SKREEE...

Dr. Mei Lin — Ellie and Danny's mother

Morning, Cam. Great to see you!

Morning, Dr. Lin!

Can you two show Cam where to get breakfast? Then we can go over today's schedule.

Hi, Cleo! This is Cam. He's new here.

Hi, Cam. Hi, kids!

I'm Cleo, one of the entomologists working here.

That means she studies insects and things.

Just a single yellow meranti tree provides a home for up to 1,000 species of insects, fungi and plants.

Rare animals of Borneo

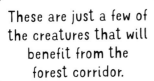

These are just a few of the creatures that will benefit from the forest corridor.

Storm's stork

The rarest stork species. It's thought there are fewer than 500 left in the wild.

Hairy-nosed otter

The world's rarest otter species, they are nearly extinct – meaning there are none left – in the wild.

Banteng

Banteng are a type of wild cattle. There are fewer than 500 left in the wild.

Helmeted hornbill

The helmeted hornbill has been hunted to the edge of extinction. No one is sure how many are left.

Bornean elephant

The smallest type of elephant. There are only around 1,500 left in the wild.

Oh, it's time to head to the boat to meet Dr. Lin!

Follow me, the jetty is this way.

Err, what's all that noise?!

SNUFFLE

SNUFFLE

GRUNT!

SNORT!

Oh, that's probably just Monty!

See! He's a bearded pig, he comes to visit a few times a week.

Sometimes we give him snacks. He likes pulasan fruit most.

Bearded pigs use their snouts to dig for roots, worms, fruit and seedlings.

At the jetty...

Hi everyone! Everything is in the boat. Ready to go up the river?

Definitely! I think I've got everything I'll need.

Jungle essentials

Head lamp
Daylight can fade fast toward the end of the day.

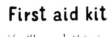

First aid kit
You'll need this in case of accidents, or even just blisters.

Hat or head covering
The sun's rays can still filter through the forest canopy and they're very strong.

Rain poncho
It rains almost every day in the jungle.

Binoculars
These are crucial for spotting wildlife in the distance.

Dry bags
Make sure electronics, notebooks and snacks are kept dry.

Towel
It's incredibly hot and humid in the jungle so you'll sweat... a lot.

Leech socks
You'll need these to protect against leeches – creatures that can latch onto your legs and suck your blood.

Insect repellent
This will keep those biting beasties away.

Water pouch
Drinking lots of water is essential in the heat.

Cam, meet some of the others working around the jungle today.

Hello!

I'm Mamat, in charge of the bird conservation team.

Hi Cam, I'm Rosli, I'll be helping you and Dr. Lin.

We'll be studying birds in the area and installing this artificial hornbill nest box.

So, Mamat, why do you need to put up nests for the hornbills?

Hornbills make nests in holes in very tall trees, but most of them have been cut down. So we've built these artificial ones to help them.

We found the perfect tree yesterday – shaded from direct sunlight...

...but tall and strong enough to withstand high winds...

...and heavy rainstorms.

16

7:30 a.m. Up the river...

Excited to go into the jungle, Cam?

Definitely! Let me just zip these on and I'm good to go!

Don't forget to put your leech socks on. You don't want anything crawling up your legs!

Make sure to tie leech socks securely. Leeches can get through very small spaces.

Look for the fluorescent yellow strips. They mark the entrances to our jungle trails.

Hey, everyone! Come look at this!

Wow! What is that?

How did you even see it?! It blends in so perfectly.

It's a type of stick insect called Chan's megastick. It's one of the longest insects in the world!

ELLIE AND DANNY'S FIELD NOTES

The Borneo rainforest is the oldest in the world. Even though over a third of it has been cut down, it is still one of the most biodiverse. Here are just some of the things that live here...

MAMMALS ←
Any animal that makes milk to feed its young.

- 222 species of mammal
- 44 found only in Borneo

Horsfields tarsier
Tarsiers are unable to move their huge eyes. Instead they must turn their head to look around.

Binturong
These rotate their hind legs to keep their grip while climbing down trees head first.

BIRDS
- 420 species of bird
- 74 found only in Borneo

Blue-winged pitta
They build messy nests on the ground.

Great argus pheasant
Males prepare a dancing ground in the forest to dance for potential mates.

These include turtles, tortoises, crocodiles, alligators, and lizards.

REPTILES

- 254 species of reptile
- 91 found only in Borneo

Cat gecko
They tend to sleep with their tails curled around them, just like cats do.

Borneo bloodsucker or green tree dragon
They don't actually suck blood, but will bite if handled.

AMPHIBIANS

← This group includes frogs, salamanders and newts.

- 149 species of amphibian
- 114 only found in Borneo

Bornean flat-headed frog
These are the world's only lungless frogs. They breathe through their skin!

Matang narrow-mouthed frog
Believe it or not, this is its actual size.

FISH

- 430 species of fish
- 160 only found in Borneo

Walking catfish
They can survive out of water and actually walk on land!

Asian arowana
These fish are really big. The largest are caught and sold as pets for up to an incredible US$20,000.

INVERTEBRATES

← Creatures without backbones, including insects, spiders and snails.

- Many thousands of invertebrates - no one knows quite how many
- At least 1,000 species of ants alone

Stalk-eyed fly
Males have eye stalks longer than their bodies.

Whip scorpion
Watch out! They spray a smelly chemical to defend themselves. It sort of smells like popcorn.

PLANTS & FUNGI

- At least 15,000 species of flowering plant
- So many species of fungi it's almost impossible to estimate

Pitcher plants
These plants catch insects to digest. Sometimes, the bigger plants can even catch lizards and rats!

Yellow bridal veil stinkhorn
YUCK! These fungi smell terrible! Like rotting meat.

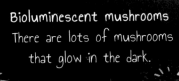

Bioluminescent mushrooms
There are lots of mushrooms that glow in the dark.

8:00 a.m. At the camera trap site...

We're here!

Great, let's get started. Cam, I'll show you what to do with the camera traps.

Camera traps are securely tied to trees.

A camera trap

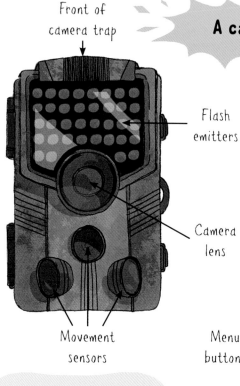

Front of camera trap

Flash emitters

Camera lens

Movement sensors

When an animal moves past the trap, movement sensors are triggered and the camera takes a picture or records a video.

Camera traps are left in the forest for weeks or even months. They help build a picture of how many different animals live in an area and how they interact.

Programming/ viewing screen

Battery compartments

Menu buttons

SD card slot

SD card – stores photos and video

Bornean orangutans

Orangutans spend most of their lives in the trees. Adults usually live alone, but their young stay with their mothers for up to eight years.

During this time they learn everything from their mothers – what to eat, how to build nests to sleep in, which animals to keep away from and how to move through the trees.

Oh, Cam, look! A trilobite beetle!

They look so ancient.

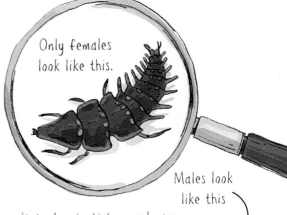

Only females look like this.

Males look like this

It took scientists nearly 100 years to find a male because they look so different.

It's err...um...

Are you ok?

Yeah, I think there's something on my...

...LEG!

Wherever you are in the jungle, blood-sucking leeches are sure to find you.

But I have leech socks on!

Hmm, looks like they don't cover that.

They can get through zippers?!

Oh yeah, they're no barrier for a leech!

Jungle bloodsuckers

Tiger leeches hang under leaves.

Common leeches live on the ground.

Leeches have heat-seeking sensors that are very sensitive to human body heat.

Try to resist pulling them off. Their mouth parts can stay attached to the skin which can cause infection.

Hi, everyone! How's the bird survey going?

We've only caught a few birds so far. The mist nets took a while to set up.

Mist nets

Mist nets are used to catch and study wild birds.

The netting is very soft and so fine that it is almost invisible when set up.

The nets have loose, baggy pockets. So, when a bird flies into the net, it will safely fall into a pocket without being injured.

Here, you can help us log what we've caught and take their measurements.

We'll add them to our field notes too!

ELLIE AND DANNY'S BIRD SURVEY

Bird surveys help scientists keep track of how many birds of different species there are in the jungle. Each bird caught has a small ring placed around its leg so can be identified next time it's caught.

	Species	Sex	Length	Weight
1	Asian paradise flycatcher	Male	20cm (8in)	20g (0.7oz)
2	Banded broadbill	Female	23cm (9in)	80g (2.8oz)
3	Dark-throated oriole	Female	18cm (7in)	38g (1.3oz)
4	Maroon woodpecker	Female	23cm (9in)	76g (2.7oz)
5	Blue-headed pitta	Male	17cm (6.5in)	72g (2.5oz)
6	Black-naped monarch	Male	16cm (6in)	10g (0.4oz)

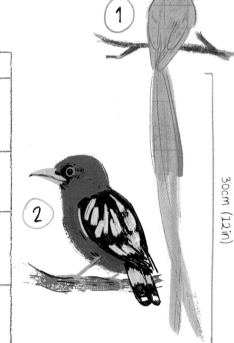

30cm (12in)

Cleo's lab...

Cleo's guide to dung beetles

Dung beetles are very sensitive to changes in the forest – the healthier the forest, the more species of dung beetle you'll find.

Dung beetles feed on animal dung, and lay eggs in it. Many – known as *rollers* – roll the dung into a ball. Others, called *tunnellers*, bury it and a third group, known as *dwellers*, just live in it.

Dung beetles are vital to a healthy forest.

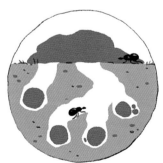

They allow air into the soil and improve water drainage by digging tunnels.

They help plants grow by recycling nutrients from the dung into the soil...

...and by spreading seeds, rolled up with the dung, far and wide.

ELLIE'S GUIDE TO THE BUGS AND INSECTS WE LIKE BEST

I **(Ellie)** like anything sneaky or gruesome or that camouflages itself.

Ninja slug
Only found in Borneo, these fire harpoons known as "love darts" at potential mates.

Bird-dropping crab spider
When curled up, these look like bird droppings - which helps them avoid being eaten. They even smell like bird dung!

Broad-headed bark spider
This spider wraps its legs around branches to blend in and hide from predators.

Assassin bug
This bug hunts ants, injecting them with a chemical to dissolve their insides for eating. It then attaches the bodies to its back - like a fancy coat.

Kai prefers bees and anything that looks like a flower, but absolutely NO spiders.

Blue-banded bee
Not all bees are yellow and black! But just like any other bee, blue-banded ones move from flower to flower helping to spread pollen.

Orchid mantis
These praying mantises look just like an orchid flower.

Danny loves everything bright and beautiful!

Jungle jade butterfly
All the tiny green dots on this butterfly's wings look like hundreds of glowing green stars.

Giant stink bug
Adults are green and look very different from nymphs (young) which are red - but they're all bright and beautiful.

Leaf butterfly
When its wings are closed, this butterfly looks like a dry dead leaf. When they're open, you'd never guess it was such a master of disguise.

Wings closed

Wings open

Jade green cicada
One of the most beautiful cicadas you will see - its blue-veined wings are almost totally see-through.

Cleo loves ALL bugs and insects - these are just a few she's mentioned.

Tortoise beetles
These beetles look a little like tortoises. Some species have clear outer shells that cover their legs.

Violin beetle
A big violin-shaped beetle. These produce a noxious, stinging fluid if threatened.

Exploding ant
When these ants feel threatened, they squeeze their muscles so hard they explode, leaving behind a toxic, sticky, yellow goo.

Long-jawed orb weaver
The red and blue body looks amazingly metallic.

Direct heat, being shaken or blown on will also cause the leaves to fold inward.

Sunda clouded leopard

Clouded leopards are named after their large, cloud-like markings.

Clouded leopard skull

Canine teeth

They have the longest canine teeth - compared to the size of their skulls - of any living cat species.

Clouded leopards spend a lot of time up in the trees. They have rotating ankle joints that allow them to climb down trees head-first.

Their long teeth help them grab their prey.

Yes! We have a clouded leopard.

I'll check that it looks healthy and isn't too old to be tranquillised.

Tranquillising means putting animals to sleep for a short time. This allows scientists to examine them safely.

Everything looks good. It's a young female, very healthy looking.

Great, we'll set up while you tranquillise her.

Tranquilliser guns shoot needle-tipped darts filled with a safe dose of tranquilliser.

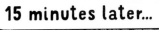

15 minutes later...

OK, she weighs 13 kilograms.

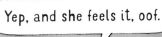

Yep, and she feels it, oof.

Wow, just over 28 pounds! That's a good weight.

Head to base of tail is 84cm or 33 inches...

This device monitors the heart rate to make sure it is steady.

...and base of tail to tip is 71cm, so 28 inches.

Canine teeth are 5cm or 2 inches.

How's she doing Hari, all good?

Heartbeat is good; temperature is normal.

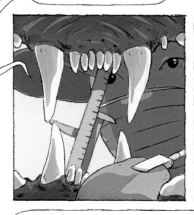

Body temperature must be monitored as well.

Ok, I'm done for now. Hari, you can take a blood sample.

Sure, this won't take a second, then we can attach the GPS collar.

A small patch of fur is shaved so blood samples can be taken to check the overall health of an animal in detail.

GPS collaring

GPS (global positioning system) uses satellites to pinpoint the location of things anywhere in the world.

GPS collars allow scientists to locate animals in the wild. The collars aren't permanent though, they're designed to fall off after a while.

6:00 p.m.

9:00 p.m. Back at the moth trap

Wow, look at all those moths!

Moon moth – these have no mouth parts and only live for around two weeks.

Atlas moth – the biggest moth in the world, it has a wingspan of 27cm (10.6 inches) wide.

It's not just moths that are attracted to the moth trap, lots of other insects are too, like this three-horned stag beetle.

Tarsolepis sommeri – these have been seen drinking mammal tears.

Oriental death's-head hawkmoth – these love honey. They can make themselves smell like bees so they can sneak into hives and steal honey.

This atlas moth is incredible. The tips of its wings look like snake heads.

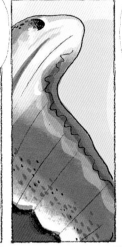

They do! If a predator threatens them they drop to the floor and slowly flap their wings to copy the head and neck movement of a snake.

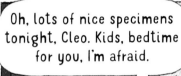

Oh, lots of nice specimens tonight, Cleo. Kids, bedtime for you, I'm afraid.

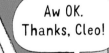

Aw OK. Thanks, Cleo!

Night, Cam!

Sleep well, see you tomorrow.

9:30 p.m.

YAWN

I can't wait for tomorrow. Goodnight, Ma.

Sleep well.

Smith's green-eyed gecko – one of the biggest
geckos in the world at 35cm (14in) long

Long-tailed
macaque

GLOSSARY

This glossary explains some of the words used in this book.
Words written in *italic* type have their own entries.

BIODIVERSITY – The variety of plant and animal *species* living in a particular place.

BIOLUMINESCENCE – The ability of some living things to make their own light.

CAMERA TRAP – A camera that is automatically triggered when something – such as an animal – moves in front of it.

CANOPY – The top layer of leaves and branches in a *rainforest*.

CONSERVATION – The effort to protect and preserve animals and the places where they live.

ENTOMOLOGY – The study of insects.

EXTINCTION – When the last member of a *species* dies, that species is extinct.

EYESHINE – The glow that some animals' eyes have in the dark when light is reflected off them.

FLUORESCENCE – Light given off by certain substances when they absorb light such as UV.

FOREST CORRIDOR – An area of trees planted to connect separate parts of a forest, allowing animal populations to move freely between them.

GPS COLLAR – A device that allows scientists to pinpoint an individual animal's exact location in the wild.

JUNGLE – An area in a hot place covered with thick, impenetrable vegetation. Often used as another word for *rainforest*.

MIST NET – A very fine mesh netting used by scientists to capture and study wild birds and bats.

MOTH TRAP – A device used by *entomologists* to capture and study moths.

OIL PALM – A type of palm tree. Oil is extracted from the fruit and used in food and toiletry manufacturing. Unregulated oil palm plantations have caused great environmental damage.

PLANTATION – An area of land where a large amount of a single plant crop – such as *oil palm* – is grown.

RAINFOREST – A dense forest in a hot place that receives a lot of rain all year.

SPECIES – A particular type of animal, plant or other living thing.

TRANQUILLISER – A drug used to make an animal sleepy or unconscious for a short while.

INDEX

First published in 2022 by Usborne Publishing Ltd.,
Usborne House, 83-85 Saffron Hill, London EC1N 8RT, United Kingdom. usborne.com
Copyright © 2022 Usborne Publishing Ltd. The name Usborne and the Balloon logo are Trade Marks of Usborne Publishing Ltd.
All rights reserved. No part of this publication may be reproduced, stored in any retrieval system, or transmitted
in any form or by any means, without the prior permission of the publisher. Printed in UAE. UKE.

Usborne Publishing is not responsible and does not accept liability for the availability or content of any website other than its own,
or for any exposure to harmful, offensive or inaccurate material which may appear on the Web. Usborne Publishing will have no
liability for any damage or loss caused by viruses that may be downloaded as a result of browsing the sites it recommends.